UNDER THE MICROSCOPE

Muscles

How we move and exercise

Richard Walker

W

FRANKLIN WATTS

LONDON•SYDNEY

ABOUT THIS BOOK

First published in 1998
This edition 2001

Franklin Watts
96 Leonard Street
London EC2A 4XD

Franklin Watts Australia
56 O'Riordan Street
Alexandria
NSW 2015

© Franklin Watts 1998

0 7496 3082 5 (Hardback)
0 7496 4399 4 (Paperback)

Dewey Decimal Classification Number: 611

A CIP catalogue record for this book is
available from the British Library

Printed in Belgium

Under the Microscope uses micro-photography to allow you to see right inside the human body.

The camera acts as a microscope, looking at unseen parts of the body and zooming in on the body's cells at work. Some micro-photographs are magnified hundreds of times, others thousands of times. They have been dramatically coloured to bring details into crisp focus, and are linked to clear and accurate illustrations that fit them in context inside the body.

New words are explained the first time that they are used, and can also be checked in the glossary at the back of the book.

Produced for Franklin Watts
by Miles Kelly Publishing
Unit 11
The Bardfield Centre
Great Bardfield
Essex
CM7 4SL

Designed by Full Steam Ahead

Illustrated by Guy Smith,

Mainline Design

Artwork commissioned
by Branka Surla

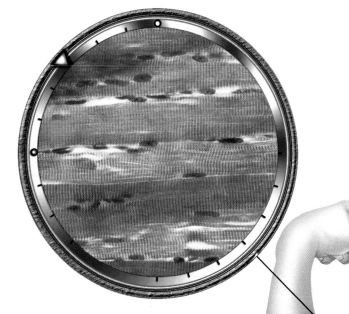

Pullers and movers
Your body is moved by muscles. Under a powerful microscope (top) you can see that muscles are made up of long stripy cells (above). These cells have an unusual ability – they can get shorter and pull on the bones of the skeleton to make the body move. Thanks to these 'pullers' you can walk, write, dance, sing and perform many other actions.

CONTENTS

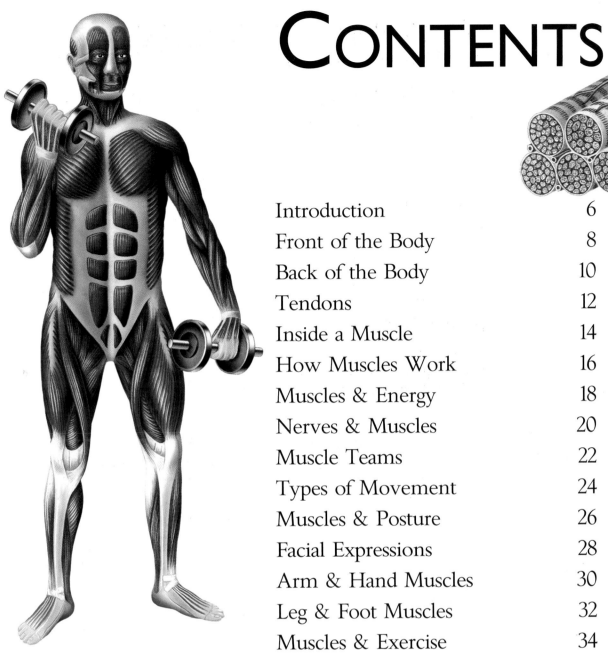
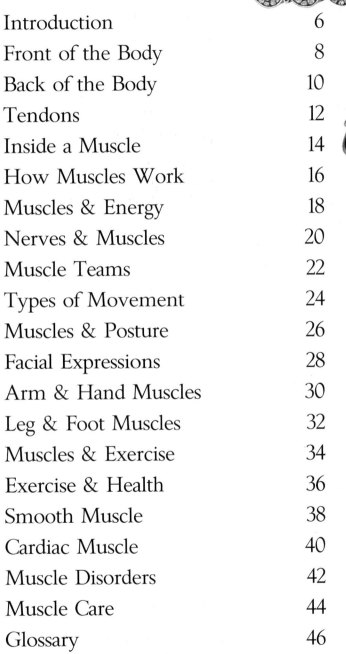
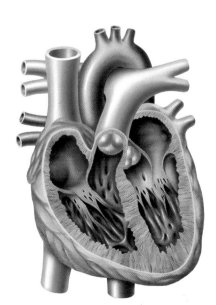

INTRODUCTION

All human activities — smiling at a friend, running for a bus, writing a note, standing up straight, swallowing food and the regular beating of the heart — have something in common. These, and many other body movements, depend on the action of body tissues called muscles.

Muscles have the unique ability to contract — or get shorter — and then relax and return to their original length. By getting shorter — an action that requires energy — muscles are able to move parts of the body. They bend and straighten our legs when we run, and squeeze our oesophagus (the tube that links the throat to the stomach) when we swallow food.

There are three types of muscles found inside the body. The bulk of the body's muscles are skeletal muscles. These pull on bones to move us around. They are the muscles that 'bulge' when a body-builder poses. Smooth muscles are found in the walls of the body's hollow organs, such as the bladder. They perform automatic tasks such as making blood vessels narrower, or propelling food along the intestines. Cardiac muscle forms the non-stop, hard-working pump, the heart, which moves blood around the body. This volume of **Under the Microscope** focuses on the body's muscles to see what they do and how they work.

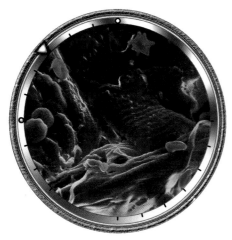

Supporting fibres

These yellow ribbons are fibres of collagen. These tough but flexible fibres form part of the supporting sheath that surrounds muscle cells. These sheaths help to hold the whole muscle together.

Blood supply

Snaking through the muscle in the main picture on the right is a tiny blood vessel. Blood in vessels like this supplies all muscle cells with food and oxygen. These provide muscles with the energy they need.

Nerve meets muscle

This micrograph (left) shows the junction between a nerve cell and a muscle cell. Nerve messages are carried by nerve cells from the brain to the muscle. When the message arrives at the junction, the muscle cell contracts.

Muscle cells

Like other body tissues and organs, muscles are made of cells. Here you can see details of the inside of a muscle cell. These are the long thin myofibrils that fill the muscle cell and give it its striped appearance.

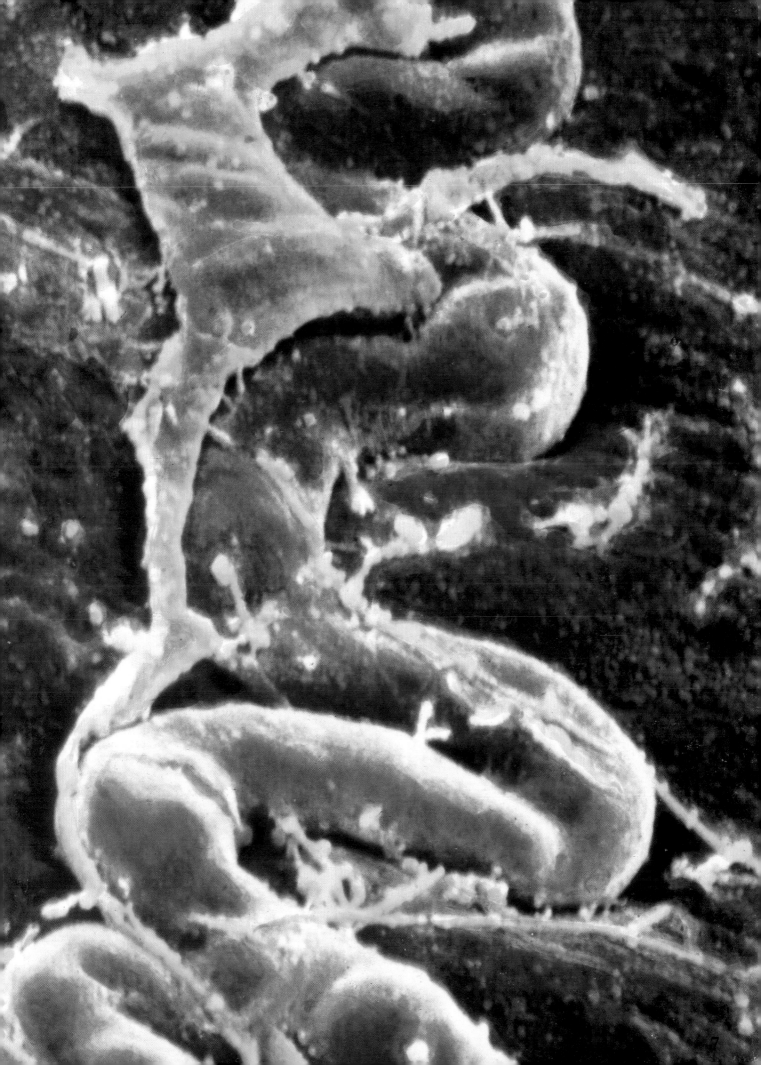

FRONT OF THE BODY

Skeletal muscles (so called because they move and support the skeleton) form up to 50 per cent of your body's weight. There are about 640 individually named skeletal muscles in the body.

Muscles cover the framework formed by the bony skeleton to give the body its shape. Where the bones of the skeleton meet, they form joints, most of which are movable. A skeletal muscle links two bones and passes across the joint between them. When the muscle contracts, or shortens, the bones move.

Muscles are arranged in layers over the skeleton. Those nearest to the skin are called superficial muscles, while the layers closer to the inside of the body are called deep muscles. Muscles are given names, usually in Latin, that may describe the shape, location, or the job of the muscle.

The skeletal muscles of the front of the body are described here. Those of the back of the body are described on the next pages.

Body movers

This micrograph shows part of the muscles of the shoulder that run from the arm to the shoulder blade.

Muscle man

A karate expert concentrates to use the force of his arm muscles to smash through these blocks. Compare the muscle outlines you see on this real person, with the muscles drawn on the opposite page.

Stripy cells

These long cylinders are muscle cells or muscle fibres. They run in parallel along the length of the muscle. Inside each fibre are more tiny cylinders called myofibrils. They give the fibre its stripy appearance.

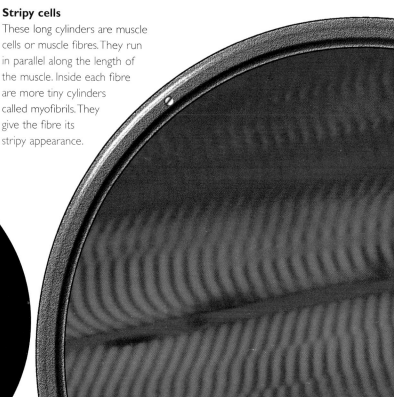

Muscles of the front of the body

If we could strip the skin and fat from the front of the body you would see the superficial skeletal muscles shown here. Each of the muscles has one or more specific jobs. Usually each muscle works in partnership with other muscles. The names and functions of some superficial muscles are described here.

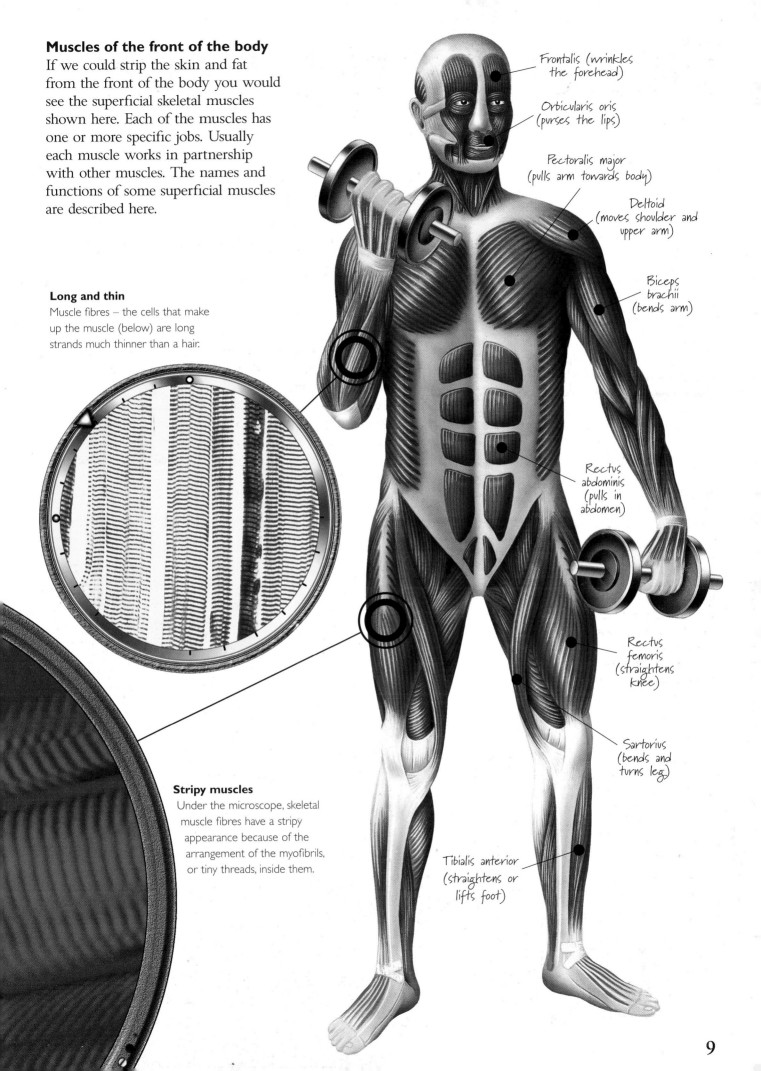

Frontalis (wrinkles the forehead)

Orbicularis oris (purses the lips)

Pectoralis major (pulls arm towards body)

Deltoid (moves shoulder and upper arm)

Biceps brachii (bends arm)

Rectus abdominis (pulls in abdomen)

Rectus femoris (straightens knee)

Sartorius (bends and turns leg)

Tibialis anterior (straightens or lifts foot)

Long and thin

Muscle fibres – the cells that make up the muscle (below) are long strands much thinner than a hair.

Stripy muscles

Under the microscope, skeletal muscle fibres have a stripy appearance because of the arrangement of the myofibrils, or tiny threads, inside them.

9

BACK OF THE BODY

Skeletal muscles are also known as voluntary muscles because you can choose – or volunteer – to make them contract. If you decide to lift your arm, your brain sends out instructions, and your muscles move your arm.

With more complicated movements – such as during walking or running – the brain sends out instructions automatically to make sure that the right muscles contract at the right time. This ensures that, without you having to think about it, you move smoothly and do not fall over.

Muscle size varies greatly. The largest and strongest muscle is the gluteus maximus in the buttocks, which is used in climbing and running. The smallest muscle, the stapedius, is just 1 millimetre (0.04 inch) long and is concealed inside the ear, where it prevents very loud sounds damaging the ear's inner mechanism.

The ancient Romans used the word musculus, which means 'little mouse', for muscles. How did that name arise? Look at the upper part of your arm, and then bend and straighten your arm at the elbow. As you do this, you should see the biceps muscle at the front of the upper arm 'move' under the skin, as it pulls on the bones of your forearm. To the ancient Romans this movement resembled a little mouse scurrying beneath the skin, hence the name.

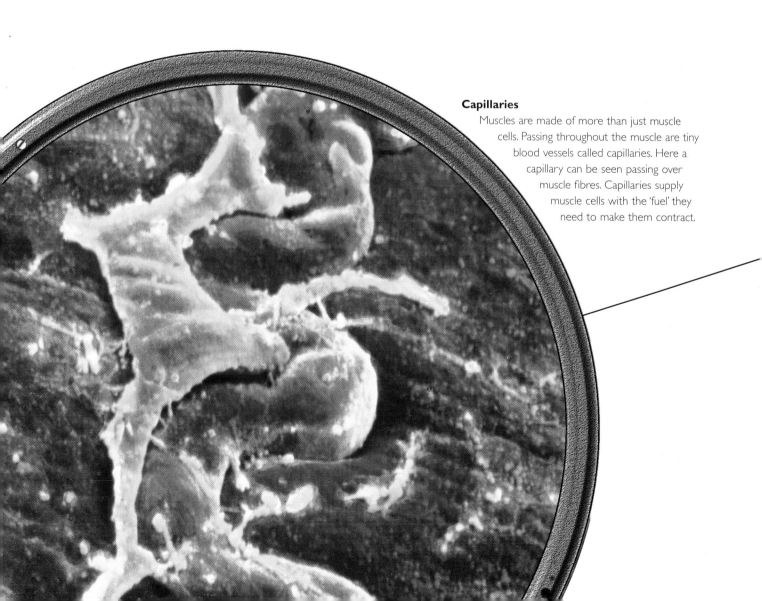

Capillaries
Muscles are made of more than just muscle cells. Passing throughout the muscle are tiny blood vessels called capillaries. Here a capillary can be seen passing over muscle fibres. Capillaries supply muscle cells with the 'fuel' they need to make them contract.

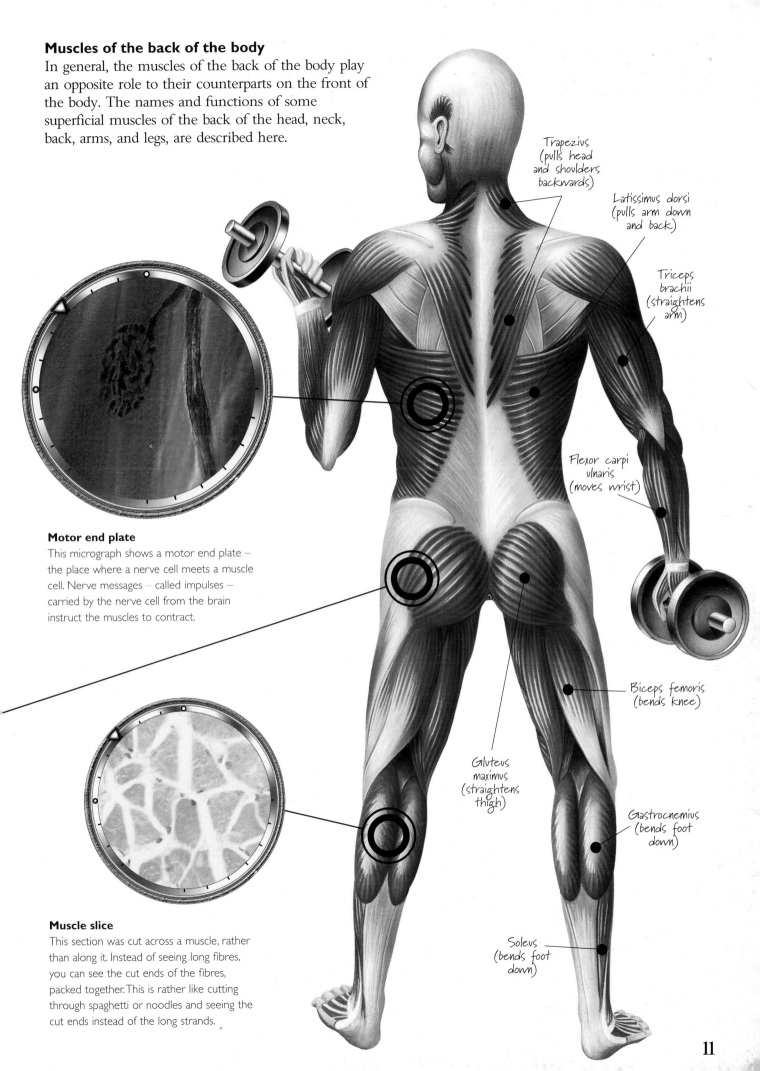

Muscles of the back of the body

In general, the muscles of the back of the body play an opposite role to their counterparts on the front of the body. The names and functions of some superficial muscles of the back of the head, neck, back, arms, and legs, are described here.

Motor end plate

This micrograph shows a motor end plate – the place where a nerve cell meets a muscle cell. Nerve messages – called impulses – carried by the nerve cell from the brain instruct the muscles to contract.

Muscle slice

This section was cut across a muscle, rather than along it. Instead of seeing long fibres, you can see the cut ends of the fibres, packed together. This is rather like cutting through spaghetti or noodles and seeing the cut ends instead of the long strands.

Trapezius (pulls head and shoulders backwards)

Latissimus dorsi (pulls arm down and back)

Triceps brachii (straightens arm)

Flexor carpi ulnaris (moves wrist)

Biceps femoris (bends knee)

Gluteus maximus (straightens thigh)

Gastrocnemius (bends foot down)

Soleus (bends foot down)

11

TENDONS

Put the fingers of your right hand in the bend of your left elbow. You should be able to feel something firm, like a thick cord. Try bending and straightening your arm and you will be able to feel it more easily. Now feel the back of one ankle. You should be able to feel an even thicker 'cord' there. Lift the back of your foot and it should be even more obvious. In both cases — elbow and ankle — you are feeling tendons.

What are tendons? They are tough tissues found at each end of a muscle. Their job is to connect muscles to bones. When a muscle contracts it pulls a bone by its tendon, just as a tow truck pulls on a broken-down car with a chain or rope. Many tendons — like the ones you felt — are shaped like cables. Some of these cable-shaped tendons are very long. Look at the back of your hand and wiggle your fingers: you will see the tendons that connect the muscles in your arm to the bones in your fingers. Other tendons are broad and flat. These tendons not only link muscles to bones; some may also connect one muscle to another.

Inside a tendon
A microscopic view inside a tendon (above) reveals bundles of collagen fibres running parallel to each other and in the same direction as the muscle. These collagen 'mini-cables' — shown here cut across — give the tendon its great strength.

Achilles tendon
A section through the Achilles tendon (below) shows bundles of collagen fibres. This tendon attaches the calf muscles to the heel bone. When the calf muscles contract they make the foot point downwards.

Muscles and tendons
Look at the end of a muscle under the microscope and you can see where muscle and tendon merge. In the lower part of this micrograph are muscle fibres, while in the upper part are the bundles of collagen fibres that form the tendon.

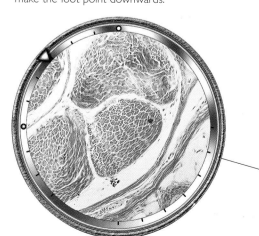

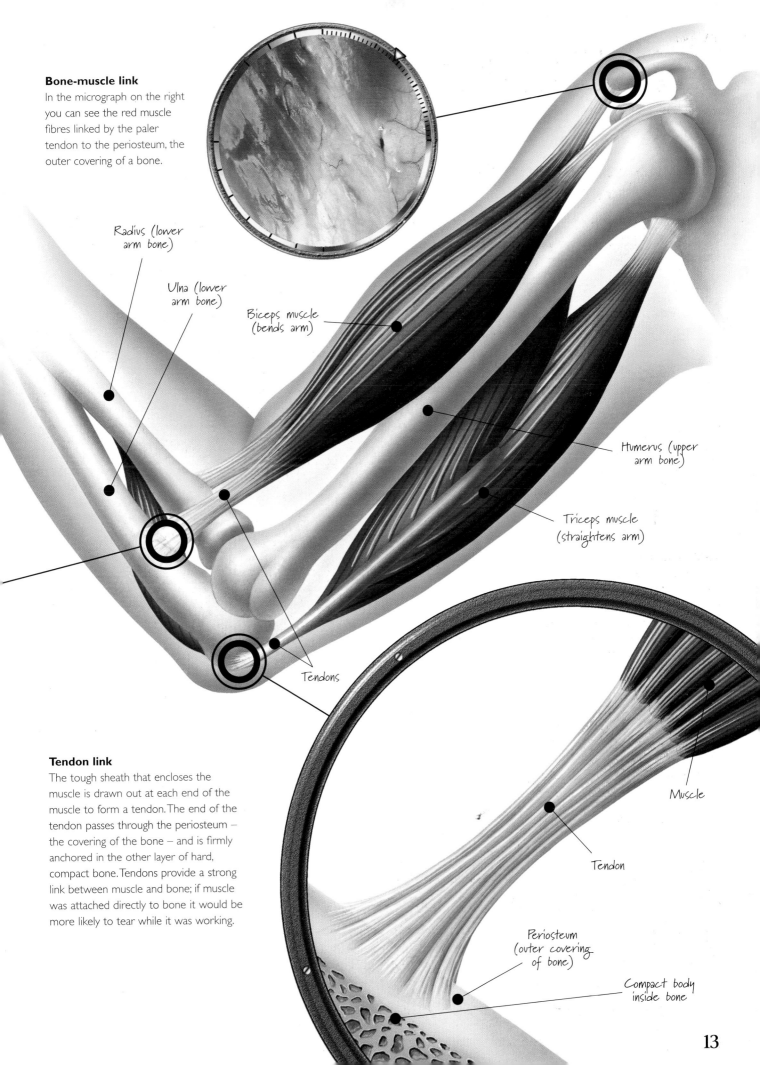

Bone-muscle link
In the micrograph on the right you can see the red muscle fibres linked by the paler tendon to the periosteum, the outer covering of a bone.

Radius (lower arm bone)

Ulna (lower arm bone)

Biceps muscle (bends arm)

Humerus (upper arm bone)

Triceps muscle (straightens arm)

Tendons

Muscle

Tendon

Periosteum (outer covering of bone)

Compact body inside bone

Tendon link
The tough sheath that encloses the muscle is drawn out at each end of the muscle to form a tendon. The end of the tendon passes through the periosteum – the covering of the bone – and is firmly anchored in the other layer of hard, compact bone. Tendons provide a strong link between muscle and bone; if muscle was attached directly to bone it would be more likely to tear while it was working.

INSIDE A MUSCLE

Skeletal muscles vary in shape and size but all have the same basic structure. Inside, a muscle is made up of long cells called fibres. A muscle fibre can be up to 30 centimetres (1 foot) in length, but is much thinner than a hair.

When seen under the microscope, skeletal muscle fibres appear striped. For this reason, skeletal or voluntary muscle is also sometimes called striate muscle, because 'striate' is another word for striped.

Skeletal muscle fibres − the cells that make up muscles − are very different in structure from other body cells. Each fibre contains thousands of tiny strands called myofibrils that run along its length. Each myofibril is made up of filaments of protein. There are two types of filaments: thick ones, made of a protein called myosin; and thin ones made of a protein called actin. Myosin and actin interact, or act together, to make the muscle shorter. This process will be explained later in the book.

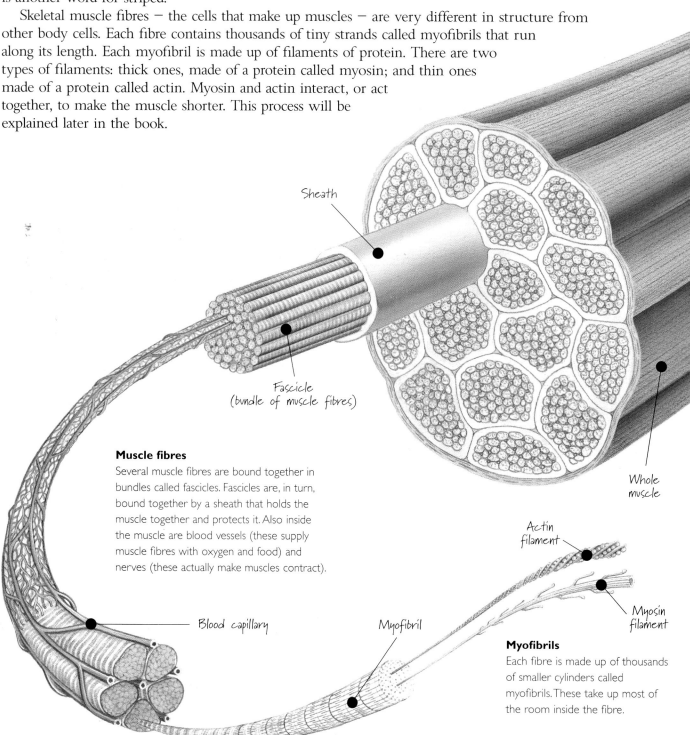

Sheath

Fascicle
(bundle of muscle fibres)

Whole muscle

Muscle fibres
Several muscle fibres are bound together in bundles called fascicles. Fascicles are, in turn, bound together by a sheath that holds the muscle together and protects it. Also inside the muscle are blood vessels (these supply muscle fibres with oxygen and food) and nerves (these actually make muscles contract).

Blood capillary

Myofibril

Actin filament

Myosin filament

Myofibrils
Each fibre is made up of thousands of smaller cylinders called myofibrils. These take up most of the room inside the fibre.

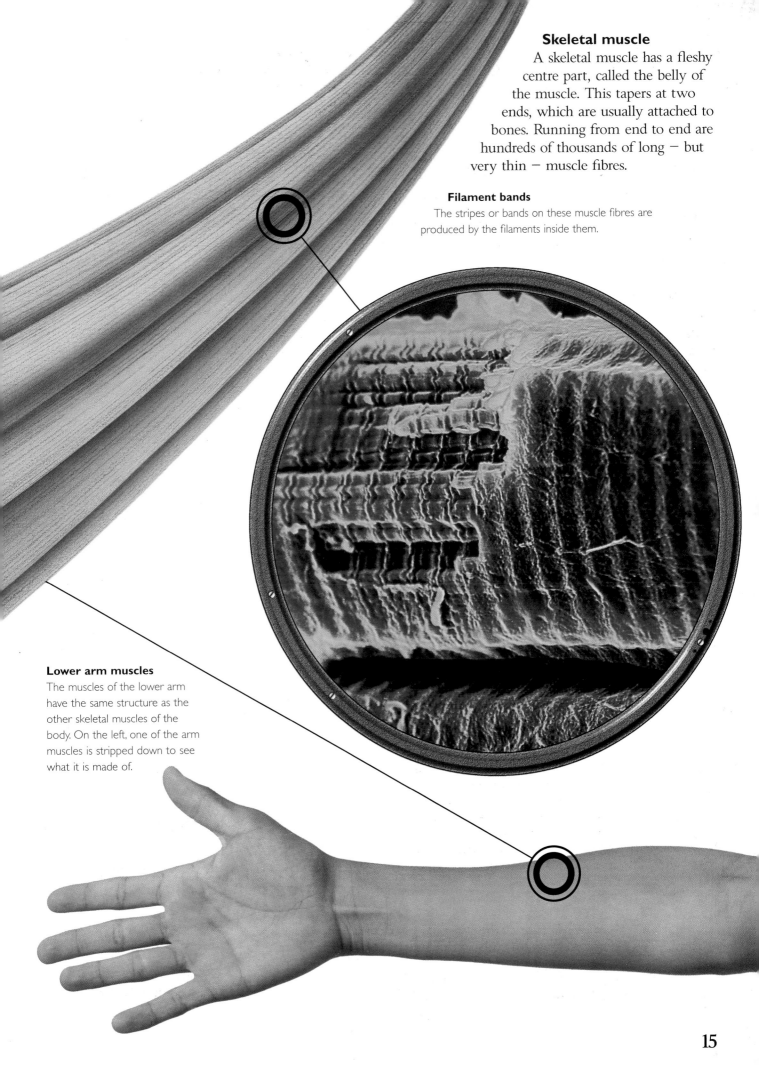

Skeletal muscle

A skeletal muscle has a fleshy centre part, called the belly of the muscle. This tapers at two ends, which are usually attached to bones. Running from end to end are hundreds of thousands of long – but very thin – muscle fibres.

Filament bands

The stripes or bands on these muscle fibres are produced by the filaments inside them.

Lower arm muscles

The muscles of the lower arm have the same structure as the other skeletal muscles of the body. On the left, one of the arm muscles is stripped down to see what it is made of.

HOW MUSCLES WORK

Muscles work by contracting or getting shorter. But how does this actually happen?

The muscle fibres that run lengthways along muscles contain thousands of cylindrical myofibrils. These run lengthways along the fibre. Inside the myofibril are thin actin filaments and thick myosin filaments. These do not run the full length of the myofibril. Instead they are arranged in small units called sarcomeres in which they overlap. The overlapping pattern of thick and thin filaments gives the myofibril its striped appearance.

When the muscle is relaxed — that means it is not contracted — the myosin and actin filaments only overlap a little. When a muscle contracts, the myosin filaments pull on the actin filaments rather like someone pulling on a rope. This makes all the sarcomeres shorter, so that the muscle contracts.

Contraction is triggered by a nerve message or impulse arriving along a nerve. But in order to contract, muscles need energy.

Biceps

Triceps

Bending the arm
Here, the upper arm muscle, the biceps, is contracting in order to bend the arm. Its fibres are getting shorter. The upper arm muscle, the triceps, is relaxed and stretching. Its fibres are getting longer.

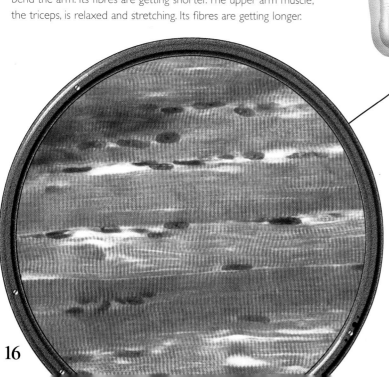

Contracting and relaxing
The micrograph above shows a contracted muscle. The muscle's banding pattern is thick. This is because the actin and myosin filaments are overlapping more than normal as they slide over each other. The micrograph on the left shows a relaxed muscle, where the muscle's banding pattern is much thinner. This is because the actin and myosin filaments are overlapping less than when the muscle is contracted.

Sliding filaments

To make a muscle contract, the myosin filaments slide between the actin filaments so that the sarcomere gets shorter. This also makes the bands or stripes come closer together. Because all the sarcomeres in a myofibril get shorter, the myofibrils themselves gets shorter. And because all the myofibrils in a muscle fibre get shorter, the muscle fibre gets shorter. When all the fibres in a muscle get shorter, the muscle contracts. Once the muscle relaxes, the actin and myosin filaments slide back to their original position.

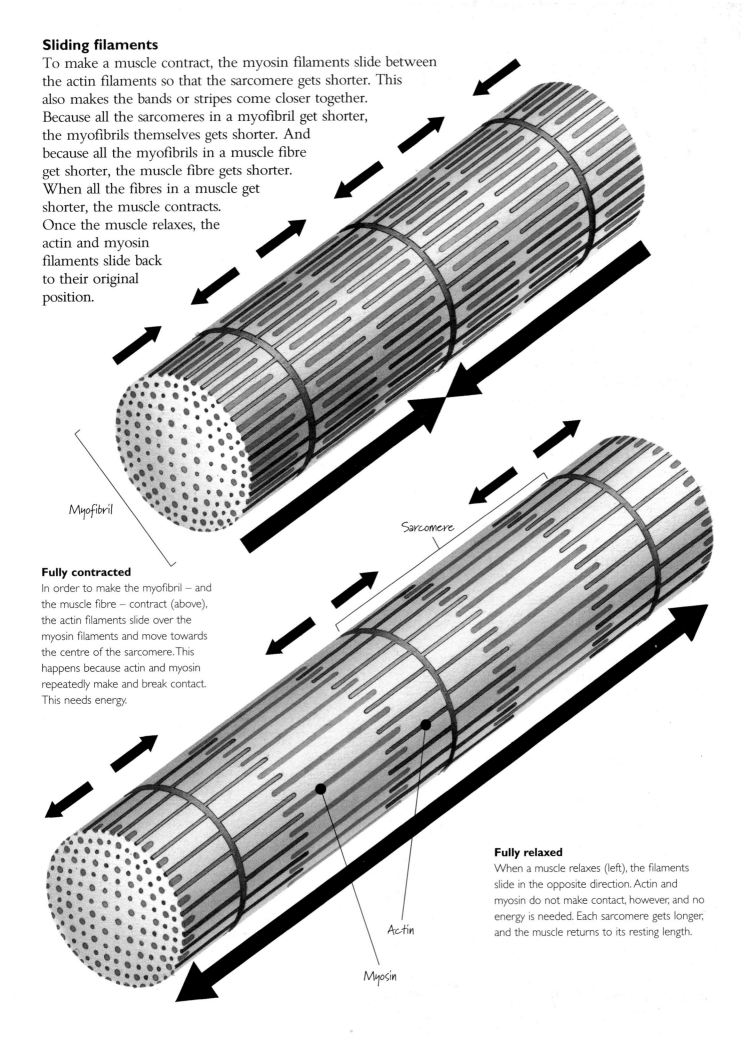

Myofibril

Fully contracted

In order to make the myofibril – and the muscle fibre – contract (above), the actin filaments slide over the myosin filaments and move towards the centre of the sarcomere. This happens because actin and myosin repeatedly make and break contact. This needs energy.

Sarcomere

Fully relaxed

When a muscle relaxes (left), the filaments slide in the opposite direction. Actin and myosin do not make contact, however, and no energy is needed. Each sarcomere gets longer, and the muscle returns to its resting length.

Actin

Myosin

MUSCLES & ENERGY

Imagine that you have been running quickly or for a long time. What would you notice? You should find that you feel warmer, and you may start to sweat. Sweating happens when the body wants to lose excess heat. Where has the extra heat come from?

Muscles need energy in order to contract. The energy required by the muscle is chemical energy in the form of food such as glucose. Inside each muscle fibre there are many tiny structures called mitochondria. These are the 'powerhouses' that convert glucose into a usable form of energy called ATP.

ATP attaches itself to myosin, providing the energy needed to pull the actin filaments and make the muscle contract. In this way, chemical energy in glucose is turned into kinetic (movement) energy. But during the conversion some energy is lost as heat. This heat helps to keep the body warm. If you exercise and use your muscles a lot, the body produces too much heat and you need to lose the excess. That is why you feel warm and sweat.

Powerhouses
This detailed micrograph inside a muscle shows not only actin and myosin filaments, but also tiny sausage-shaped structures called mitochondria. Mitochondria are the muscle's powerhouses. They release the energy needed to drive the muscle contraction.

Glucose
Glucose is an energy-rich substance taken into the body in food.

Energy release
The ingredients for energy release – glucose and oxygen – are carried to muscle fibres by the blood. Inside the muscle fibre's mitochondria, oxygen is used to unlock the energy stored in glucose and turn it into ATP. ATP is then used to make the muscle contract.

Oxygen
Oxygen is taken into the body in the air you breathe.

A mitochondrion
This mitochondrion is one of many 'powerhouses' inside a muscle fibre.

Energy
Energy is used to make muscles contract.

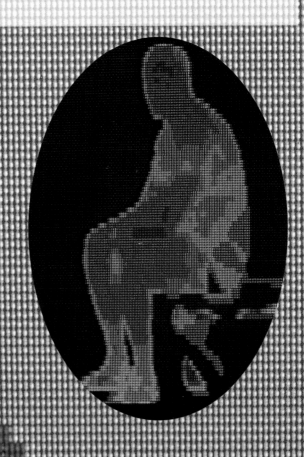

Heat pictures

These thermograms – or heat pictures – show heat being released from the body. Hot areas are white, running through yellow, red, blue, green and purple to black, the coolest. The man sitting at rest releases much less heat than the active man who is using his muscles to play squash.

NERVES & MUSCLES

Skeletal muscles will not contract on their own. They need instructions from the nervous system before they can move the body. Your nervous system controls most of your body's activities including vision, hearing, feeling and sleeping, as well as movement.

The control centre of the nervous system is the brain assisted by the spinal cord. Arising from both brain and spinal cord are nerves. These are bundles of long, narrow nerve cells, or neurons. Neurons carry electrical signals called nerve impulses to all parts of the body, including all skeletal muscles, and from all parts of the body back to the brain and spinal cord. Neurons that carry nerve impulses away from the brain and spinal cord are called motor neurons.

When you decide to move, the brain sends nerve impulses down the spinal cord and along motor neurons to the particular muscle or muscles that will produce the required movement. Motor neurons meet muscle fibres at neuromuscular ('nerve-muscle') junctions. When nerve impulses arrive at the neuromuscular junctions they spread along the muscle fibre because muscles – like nerves – can transmit electrical signals. When this happens, actin and myosin slide over each other and the muscle contracts. When the nerve impulses cease, actin and myosin return to their normal positions and the muscle relaxes.

Brain

Spinal cord

Nerve

Nervous system
The nervous system consists of the brain, the spinal cord, and the network of nerves that reaches all parts of the body. Nerves are made up of nerve cells, or neurons, that link brain and spinal cord to individual muscles.

Starter's pistol
How does the brain tell the leg muscles to move when this athlete hears the starter's pistol? Let us follow the sequence. First of all, the pistol goes off and produces a sound.

Hearing
Sound waves from the pistol travel through the air to the ear. Inside the ear they are picked up by sound detectors. These then send nerve impulses to the brain.

Control centre
Nerve impulses from the ear are interpreted as sounds in one part of the brain. A fraction of a second later, the information that a pistol shot has been heard is passed to another part of the brain. This sends out instructions down the spinal cord and along nerves that supply muscles in the legs and other parts of the body.

Where nerves meet muscles

The end of the motor neuron (seen in close-up in the micrograph on the right) divides into branches that spread over the muscle fibre. This is called a neuromuscular junction. Where the motor neuron branches and the muscle fibres meet there is a tiny gap called a synapse. When nerve impulses arrive at the end of the motor neuron, chemicals are released from the ends of the branches. These chemicals pass across the synapse, and produce a new electrical signal in the muscle fibre. This is the trigger for contraction.

The more impulses a muscle receives, the more it contracts until it reaches its minimum length. This is about 60 per cent of its relaxed length.

Nerve-muscle junction

These micrographs show exactly what a nerve-muscle – or neuromuscular – junction looks like. The string-like nerve fibre divides into separate strands. These form small swellings on the surface of the muscle fibres – which take up most of both micrographs – where muscle and nerve join.

Sprint

The runner's leg muscles contract in the right order and by the right amount to propel him forward in a sprint.

MUSCLE TEAMS

Muscles can only pull. They cannot push. For example, when the biceps contracts it pulls the forearm towards the upper arm and so bends the arm at the elbow. But the biceps cannot push the forearm away from the upper arm. So why is it that our arms are not permanently bent?

The answer lies in muscle teams. On the opposite side of the upper arm is another member of the arm-bending team. This is the triceps muscle, which pulls on the forearm so that it moves away from the upper arm and straightens the arm at the elbow. Biceps and triceps work in opposite directions and are known as antagonists because they are 'against' each other. Muscle teams are found all over the body and are responsible for all movements, even the smallest. Our brains learn to control muscle teams during the early years of life so that we can move, balance, and maintain our posture without even thinking about it.

Bending the arm
Bending and straightening the arm is just one of many examples of muscles working in opposite directions to each other. When the arm is bent at the elbow, the biceps muscle bulges as it contracts.

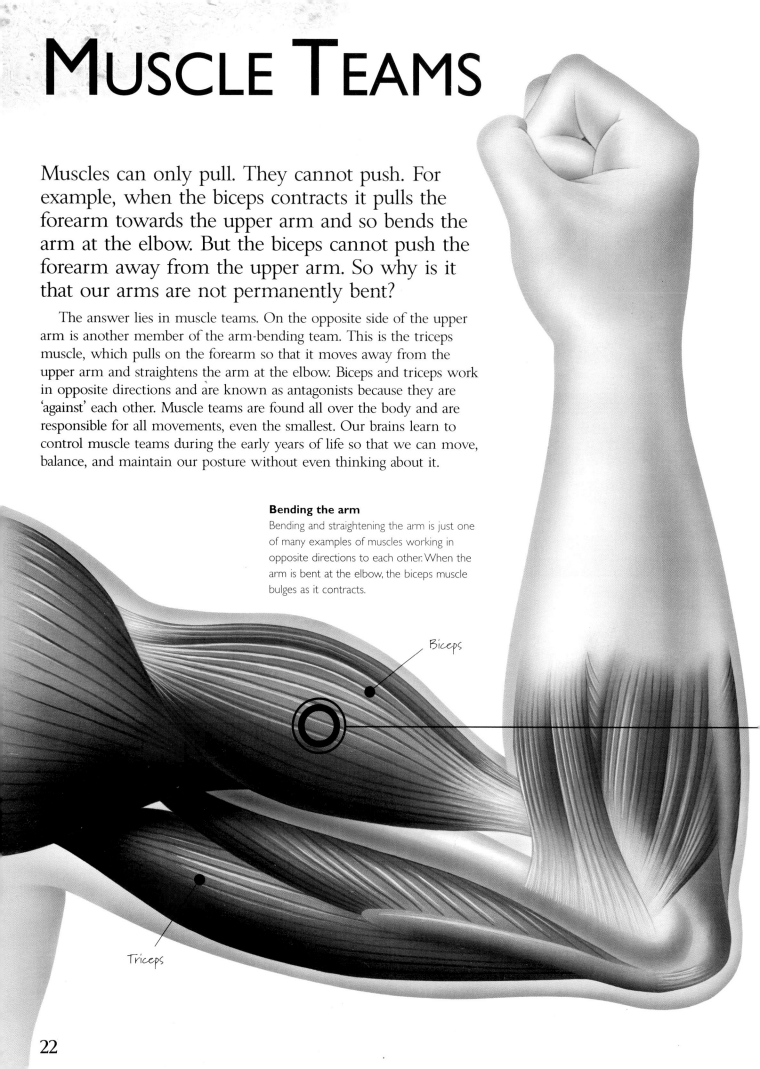

Biceps

Triceps

22

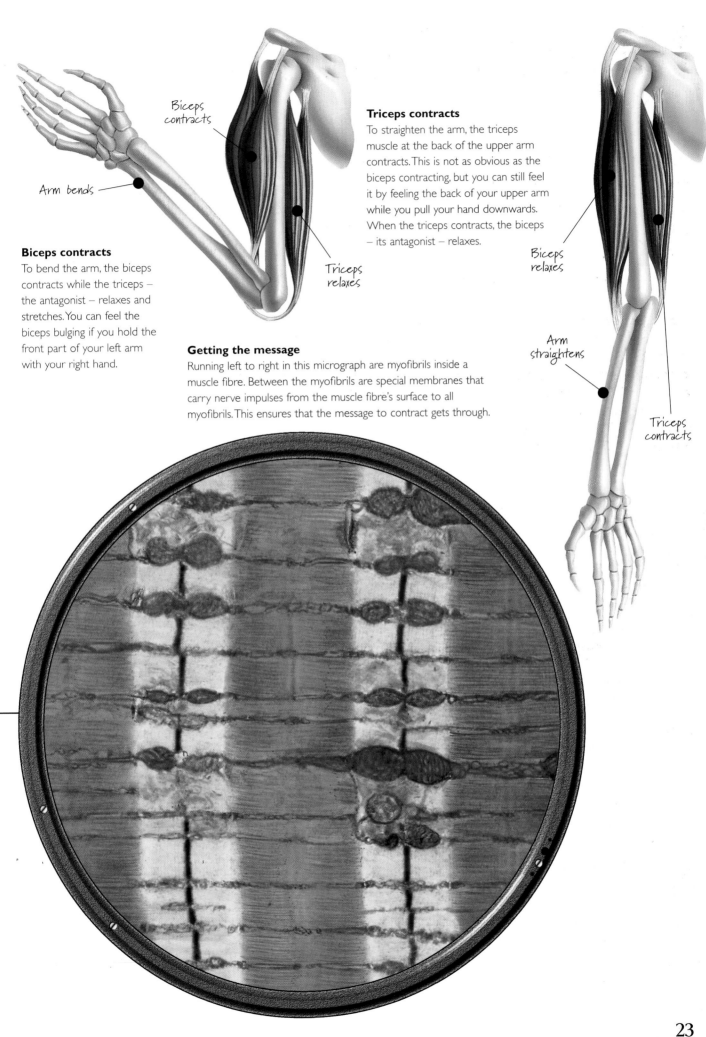

Biceps contracts

Triceps contracts
To straighten the arm, the triceps muscle at the back of the upper arm contracts. This is not as obvious as the biceps contracting, but you can still feel it by feeling the back of your upper arm while you pull your hand downwards. When the triceps contracts, the biceps – its antagonist – relaxes.

Biceps relaxes

Arm straightens

Triceps relaxes

Triceps contracts

Biceps contracts
To bend the arm, the biceps contracts while the triceps – the antagonist – relaxes and stretches. You can feel the biceps bulging if you hold the front part of your left arm with your right hand.

Arm bends

Getting the message
Running left to right in this micrograph are myofibrils inside a muscle fibre. Between the myofibrils are special membranes that carry nerve impulses from the muscle fibre's surface to all myofibrils. This ensures that the message to contract gets through.

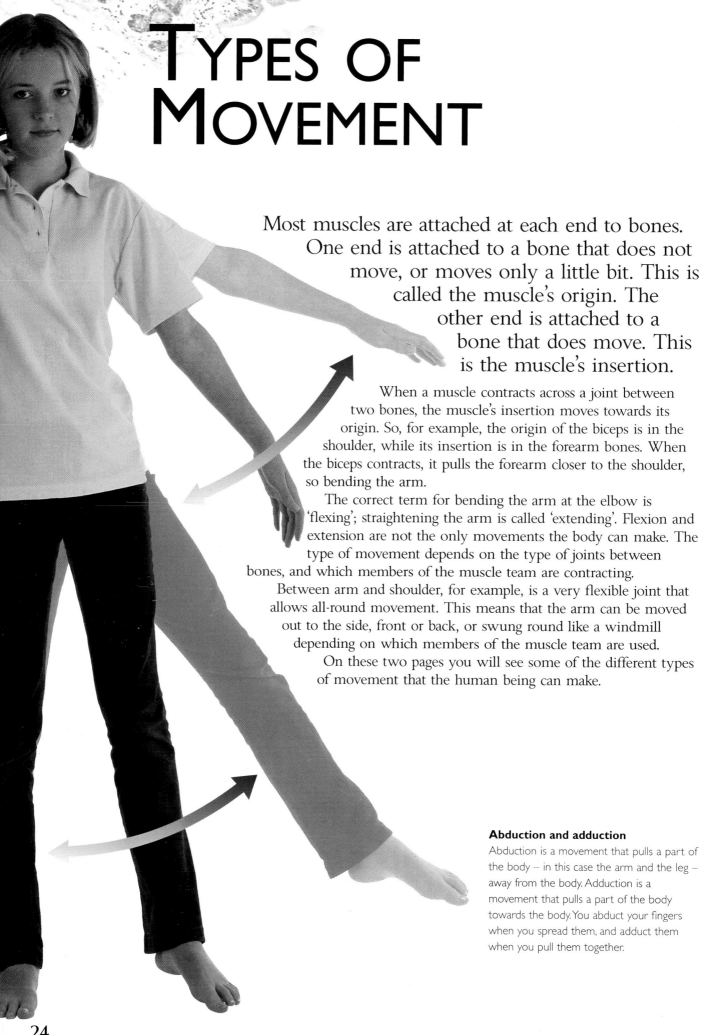

TYPES OF MOVEMENT

Most muscles are attached at each end to bones. One end is attached to a bone that does not move, or moves only a little bit. This is called the muscle's origin. The other end is attached to a bone that does move. This is the muscle's insertion.

When a muscle contracts across a joint between two bones, the muscle's insertion moves towards its origin. So, for example, the origin of the biceps is in the shoulder, while its insertion is in the forearm bones. When the biceps contracts, it pulls the forearm closer to the shoulder, so bending the arm.

The correct term for bending the arm at the elbow is 'flexing'; straightening the arm is called 'extending'. Flexion and extension are not the only movements the body can make. The type of movement depends on the type of joints between bones, and which members of the muscle team are contracting.

Between arm and shoulder, for example, is a very flexible joint that allows all-round movement. This means that the arm can be moved out to the side, front or back, or swung round like a windmill depending on which members of the muscle team are used.

On these two pages you will see some of the different types of movement that the human being can make.

Abduction and adduction
Abduction is a movement that pulls a part of the body – in this case the arm and the leg – away from the body. Adduction is a movement that pulls a part of the body towards the body. You abduct your fingers when you spread them, and adduct them when you pull them together.

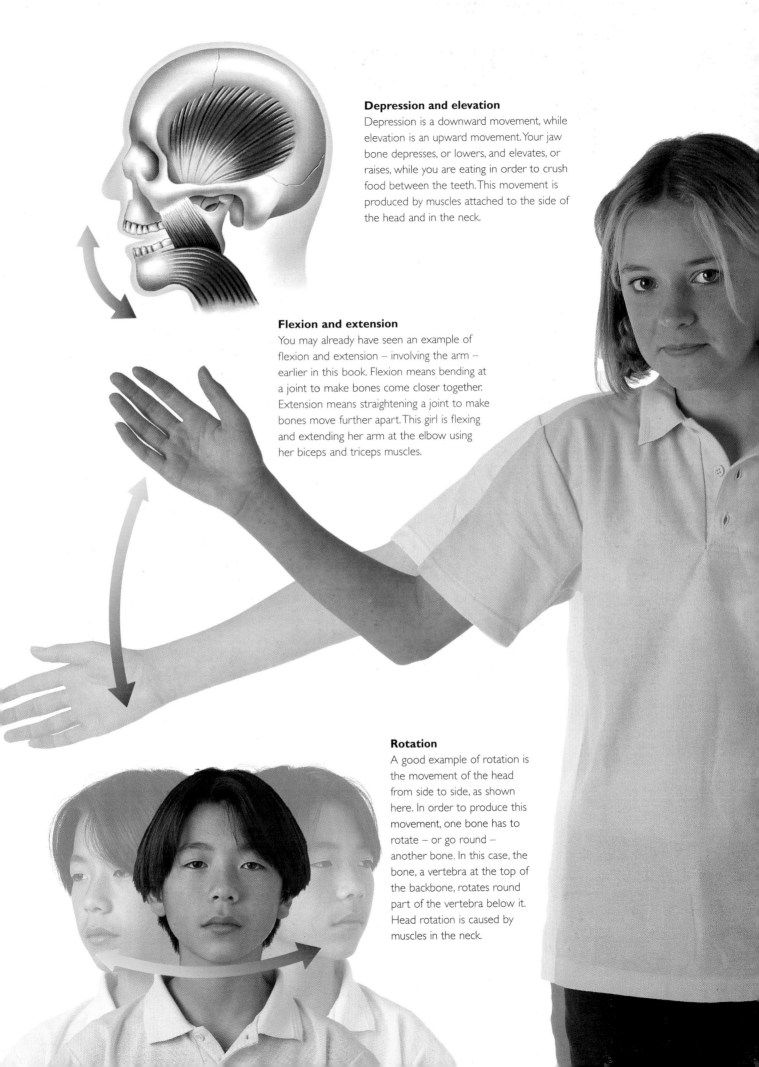

Depression and elevation

Depression is a downward movement, while elevation is an upward movement. Your jaw bone depresses, or lowers, and elevates, or raises, while you are eating in order to crush food between the teeth. This movement is produced by muscles attached to the side of the head and in the neck.

Flexion and extension

You may already have seen an example of flexion and extension – involving the arm – earlier in this book. Flexion means bending at a joint to make bones come closer together. Extension means straightening a joint to make bones move further apart. This girl is flexing and extending her arm at the elbow using her biceps and triceps muscles.

Rotation

A good example of rotation is the movement of the head from side to side, as shown here. In order to produce this movement, one bone has to rotate – or go round – another bone. In this case, the bone, a vertebra at the top of the backbone, rotates round part of the vertebra below it. Head rotation is caused by muscles in the neck.

Muscles & Posture

So far, we have looked at skeletal muscles in terms of them moving the body. But many skeletal muscles have another role to play.

When we are awake, many of our body muscles are slightly contracted. The brain sends out instructions to these muscles, making slight adjustments to their state of contraction. The muscle firmness produced is called muscle tone. This maintains our body shape and posture, enabling us to 'hold our stomachs in' and to stand or sit upright, without thinking about it. Without this mechanism your body would collapse under the influence of the Earth's gravity.

Although some muscles maintain their tone when we are asleep, most of them relax, and the body becomes more floppy. This can be seen clearly if you watch someone sitting upright who starts to fall asleep. As their muscles lose muscle tone, their head falls forwards or sideways, their arms fall to their sides, and their body slumps.

Neck muscles

The muscles at the back of the neck, and the upper back, serve to keep the head upright, and to pull it back into the upright position if it nods forwards.

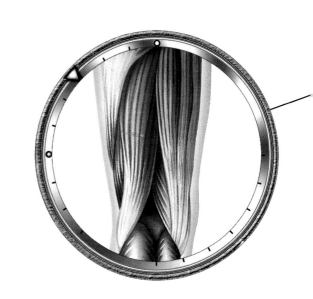

Leg muscles

The hamstring muscles at the back of the leg assist the buttock muscles in maintaining an upright posture.

Relaxed body

As we fall asleep, our muscles become more relaxed. During dreaming sleep, our muscles become 'paralysed' so that we cannot act out any parts of our dreams and possibly damage ourselves.

26

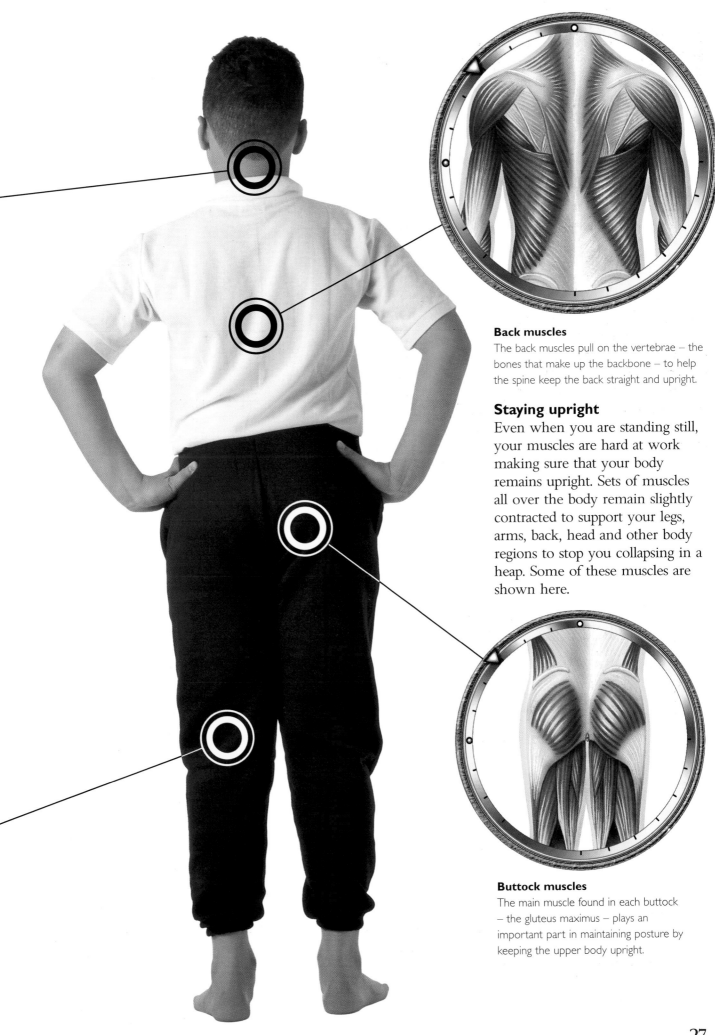

Back muscles

The back muscles pull on the vertebrae – the bones that make up the backbone – to help the spine keep the back straight and upright.

Staying upright

Even when you are standing still, your muscles are hard at work making sure that your body remains upright. Sets of muscles all over the body remain slightly contracted to support your legs, arms, back, head and other body regions to stop you collapsing in a heap. Some of these muscles are shown here.

Buttock muscles

The main muscle found in each buttock – the gluteus maximus – plays an important part in maintaining posture by keeping the upper body upright.

FACIAL EXPRESSIONS

People use different ways of communicating with each other. The most obvious is the use of words: we speak to each other in order to exchange clear messages. Another means of communication, and one that is non-verbal (without words), is the use of facial expressions.

Very small changes in the shape of our mouth, eyebrows, nose, and other parts of our face express a huge range of feelings from anger and anxiety to pleasure and surprise. The production of these facial expressions is the responsibility of a complex arrangement of small facial muscles. The 30 or so facial muscles overlay the framework provided by the facial bones of the skull.

Together, your facial bones and muscles produce the shape of your face. While most facial muscles have their origin (the point of attachment that does not move) in the skull, their insertion (the point of attachment that does move) is usually in the skin of the face. This means that even a tiny contraction of a facial muscle can, by pulling on the skin, produce a subtle change in expression. Stronger contractions can flare the nostrils, pull the mouth down, or open the eyes.

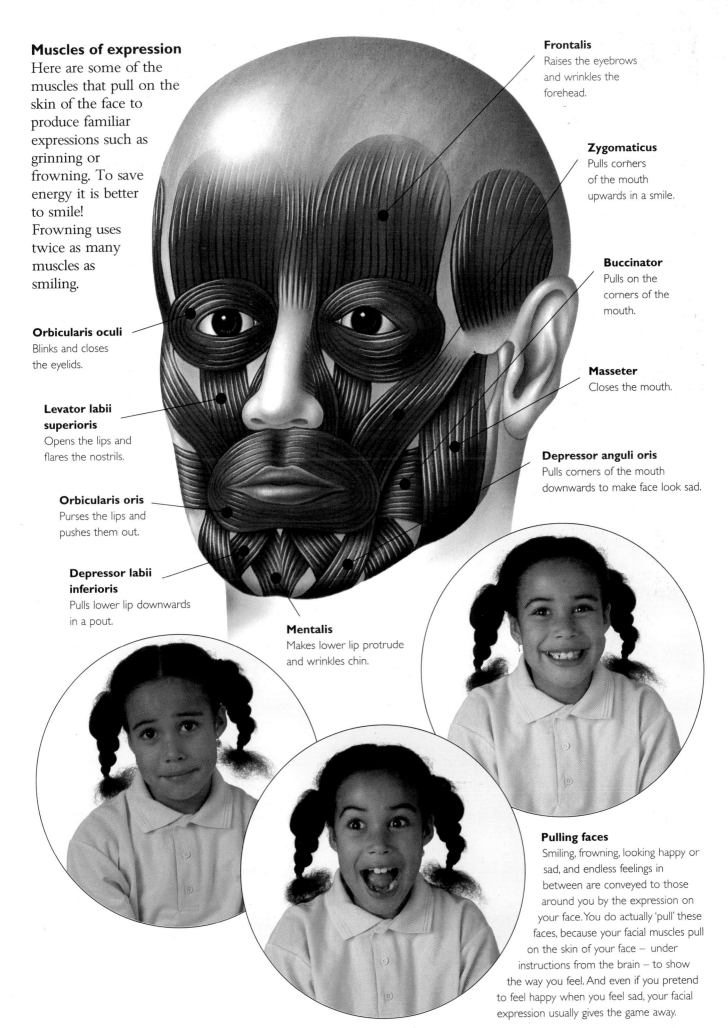

Muscles of expression

Here are some of the muscles that pull on the skin of the face to produce familiar expressions such as grinning or frowning. To save energy it is better to smile! Frowning uses twice as many muscles as smiling.

Orbicularis oculi
Blinks and closes the eyelids.

Levator labii superioris
Opens the lips and flares the nostrils.

Orbicularis oris
Purses the lips and pushes them out.

Depressor labii inferioris
Pulls lower lip downwards in a pout.

Mentalis
Makes lower lip protrude and wrinkles chin.

Frontalis
Raises the eyebrows and wrinkles the forehead.

Zygomaticus
Pulls corners of the mouth upwards in a smile.

Buccinator
Pulls on the corners of the mouth.

Masseter
Closes the mouth.

Depressor anguli oris
Pulls corners of the mouth downwards to make face look sad.

Pulling faces
Smiling, frowning, looking happy or sad, and endless feelings in between are conveyed to those around you by the expression on your face. You do actually 'pull' these faces, because your facial muscles pull on the skin of your face – under instructions from the brain – to show the way you feel. And even if you pretend to feel happy when you feel sad, your facial expression usually gives the game away.

Arm & Hand Muscles

One of the features that distinguishes humans from other animals is our ability to use our arms and hands for a whole range of different tasks.

Lifting a heavy weight, writing a letter, hitting a tennis ball, painting a picture, or hammering in a nail: all of these, and the many other tasks we perform, require the muscles of the hand and arm to work together. The hand is capable of a wide range of movement from delicate manipulation to strong grasping. The flexibility and precision of the hand is due to the intricate framework provided by the 27 hand bones; and to the many muscles of the hand and forearm.

The muscles of the hand are small and serve to flex or extend the fingers, or to move them sideways. The forearm muscles taper into long tendons that extend into the hand. If the forearm muscles themselves extended into the hand, your fingers would be very thick and unable to perform their normal activities. The long tendons pass through slippery sheaths that enable them to move smoothly when you move your fingers.

Extensor retinaculum

Tendon

Hand movements

The muscles of the lower arm and hand enable you to perform a wide range of movements. For example, you can hold a pen or chopsticks and use both with precision; you can point at an object; and you can use the hand as a hook or pincers for a firm grip.

Finger movers

Here you can see the muscles of the upper part of the left forearm and hand. Most of the muscles in this part of the arm straighten the wrist or the fingers. The long forearm muscles taper into narrow tendons that are attached to the finger bones. The extensor retinaculum is a 'wrist band' that keeps the long tendons in place.

Arms outstretched
The children here move
their arms and hands
during a gymnastic
display. They have
learned these
movements in advance.
The brain recalls them
from its memory, and
then sends instructions
to the muscles of the
arms, shoulders, chest and
back to enable each child
to perform the dance.

Trapezius

Deltoid

Traffic duty
A woman police officer
moves her right arm and
hand in order to direct the
traffic. She has learned to
make certain movements that
drivers will understand and
respond to. As she surveys the
traffic, her brain sends instructions to
her shoulder and arm muscles to produce
the movement shown here.

Shoulder and upper arm
This is a back view of the left upper arm
and shoulder. The deltoids, trapezius and
other muscles move the shoulders, and pull
the arm forwards and backwards, out to the
side, and back towards the body. The
shoulder joint is very flexible and enables
the arm to be moved in nearly all
directions. The muscles of the upper arm
bend and straighten the arm at the elbow.

LEG & FOOT MUSCLES

Put your hands on your thighs and squeeze them with your fingers. The bulk of what you can feel is made up of the large, powerful thigh muscles.

They have to be strong because we walk on two legs, and the bones and muscles of the legs have to support all our weight. Thigh muscles run from the hip bones to the lower leg, surrounding the femur, or thigh bone – the longest, strongest bone in the body. The thigh muscles flex and extend the upper part of the leg. They also pull the leg out to the side of the body and towards the body, they rotate it inwards and outwards, and they bend and straighten the leg at the knee. Thigh muscles also help to keep your body upright and maintain your posture.

The muscles of the lower leg are smaller but no less important. They serve to pull the foot upwards or downwards, and to flex and extend the toes. As in the hand and arm, these muscles taper into long tendons that extend into the foot. The foot forms a flexible platform that both supports the body and moves it by pushing the body off the ground. Together, the muscles of the thigh, lower leg, and foot enable us to walk, run, and perform a whole range of other movements.

Dancing

This dancer makes precise movements with her legs in order to produce the steps she has learned in the past. The muscles of the legs and feet enable her to produce a wide range of movements.

Running

These runners are using their leg muscles to propel themselves forward at speed. You can see their thigh muscles stiffening as they contract to bend and straighten their knees.

Front of leg

Here you can see the muscles of the front of the right leg. Upper leg muscles lift the leg at the hip, and straighten it at the knee. Lower leg muscles bend the foot upwards at the ankle and lift and straighten the toes. All of these movements form part of walking or running.

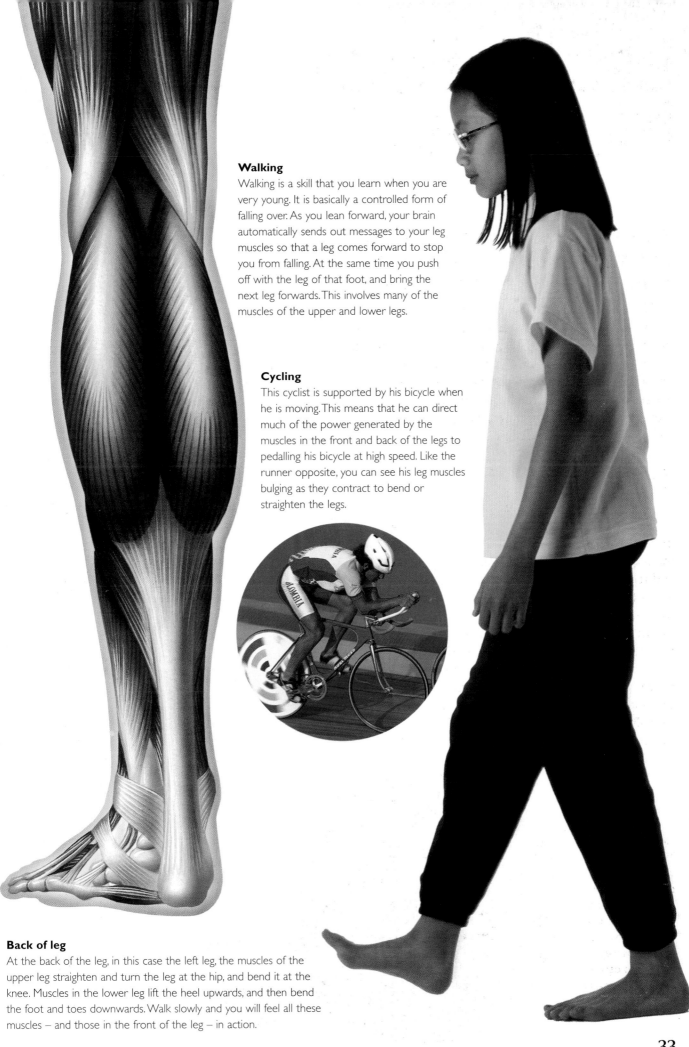

Walking

Walking is a skill that you learn when you are very young. It is basically a controlled form of falling over. As you lean forward, your brain automatically sends out messages to your leg muscles so that a leg comes forward to stop you from falling. At the same time you push off with the leg of that foot, and bring the next leg forwards. This involves many of the muscles of the upper and lower legs.

Cycling

This cyclist is supported by his bicycle when he is moving. This means that he can direct much of the power generated by the muscles in the front and back of the legs to pedalling his bicycle at high speed. Like the runner opposite, you can see his leg muscles bulging as they contract to bend or straighten the legs.

Back of leg

At the back of the leg, in this case the left leg, the muscles of the upper leg straighten and turn the leg at the hip, and bend it at the knee. Muscles in the lower leg lift the heel upwards, and then bend the foot and toes downwards. Walk slowly and you will feel all these muscles – and those in the front of the leg – in action.

MUSCLES & EXERCISE

Exercising
During exercise the muscles have to work much harder in order to move the body in the way its owner requires.

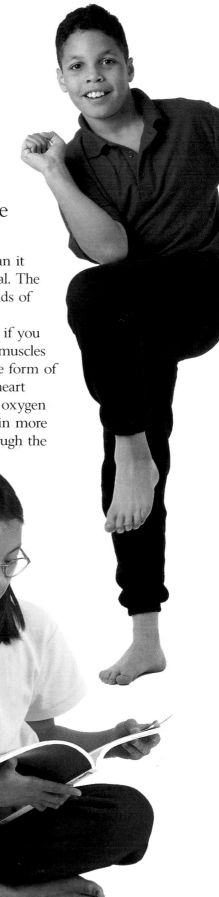

Exercise means doing something other than sitting or lying down. It could be gentle exercise, such as walking, or more vigorous exercise, such as running or playing football. Whatever the type of movement − whether gentle or vigorous − changes take place in the body as soon as you start to exercise.

Some of these changes are obvious: your heart beats faster than it would do when sitting down, and you breathe faster than normal. The reason that these changes occur is to satisfy the increased demands of your muscles. So, what are these demands?

When you exercise, you move more parts of your body than if you are at rest, and move them faster. This means that your skeletal muscles have to work harder. To work harder they need more fuel, in the form of glucose, and more oxygen to release energy from the fuel. The heart automatically beats faster to pump blood containing glucose and oxygen more rapidly to the muscles. You breathe faster in order to take in more oxygen from the air. In addition, the blood vessels that pass through the muscles actually get wider so that blood flow to the muscles increases.

At rest
When you sit down, some muscles are still working to maintain your posture, but they do not use much energy.

34

Blood flow at rest

This chart shows how much blood every minute goes to each part of the body when a person is resting. At rest – if you are sitting down, for example – muscles do not require very much energy.

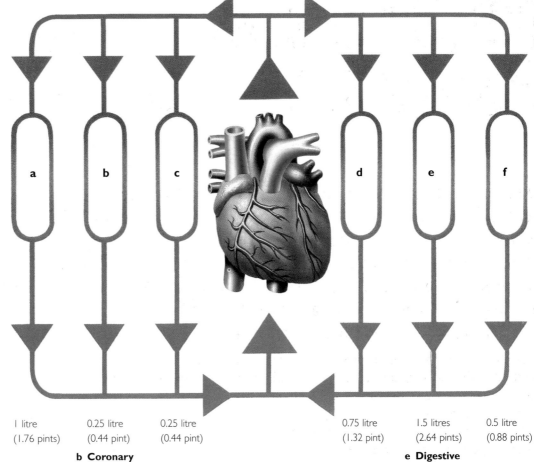

a	b	c	d	e	f
1 litre (1.76 pints)	0.25 litre (0.44 pint)	0.25 litre (0.44 pint)	0.75 litre (1.32 pint)	1.5 litres (2.64 pints)	0.5 litre (0.88 pints)
a Muscles	**b Coronary arteries of heart**	**c Brain**	**d Kidneys**	**e Digestive system and liver**	**f Skin**
12 litres (21.12 pints)	0.75 litre (1.32 pints)	0.25 litre (0.44 pint)	0.75 litre (1.32 pints)	0.5 litre (0.88 pints)	2 litres (3.52 pints)

Blood flow during exercise

During strenuous exercise, the amount of blood flowing through the body's skeletal muscles increases dramatically. Increased blood flow supplies muscles with the food and oxygen they need to provide the energy for contraction.

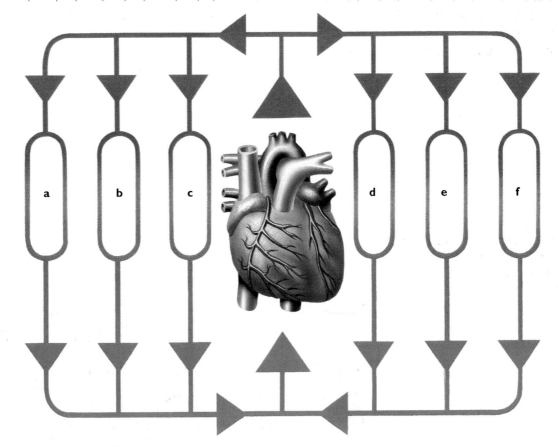

EXERCISE & HEALTH

Being active and taking exercise is something that is natural for human beings. Our distant ancestors, thousands of years ago, would have exercised every day as they built their homes and looked for food.

In the modern world, many people – both young and old – take very little exercise because they travel by car and spend a lot of time sitting in front of television or computers. But doctors have shown that exercise is very important for our well-being. Regular exercise improves fitness. This is the ability to perform an activity without getting unduly breathless. It also improves our health and lessens the chances of us becoming ill.

Exercise has several effects on the body. Firstly, it improves cardiovascular endurance or stamina. This is the ability of the heart to work efficiently over an extended period of time. Secondly, it improves muscular fitness and strength. Finally, it improves the flexibility of the body. This is the ability of the joints between bones to be moved freely by the muscles.

Different exercises contribute different effects in terms of stamina, strength and flexibility. For example, running and walking are good for stamina; weight training is good for strength; while gymnastics and yoga are good for flexibility. Exercise such as swimming and tennis is good for all three.

Running
As these runners pound round the track they are improving their endurance. Regular running exercises the heart and makes it more efficient at its job. This means it actually works less to achieve the same result.

Weight training
Weight training involves lifting weights that strengthen the muscles without straining them. Here the muscles of the upper legs, back and shoulders are being worked on.

Tennis
Tennis includes all three elements of fitness. Stamina is essential for a long match, strength is needed to serve and hit the ball, and flexibility is necessary to move the body effectively and safely around the court.

Swimming

Swimming, like tennis, is a good all-round exercise. It exercises nearly all of the body's major muscle groups, develops muscle strength and endurance, improves posture and flexibility, and places great demands on the heart, thereby increasing stamina.

Gymnastics

Gymnasts have to be lithe, supple and flexible in order to perform like this young woman. They need both strength and stamina to control their skilled movements and achieve the graceful and extreme positions required in competition.

SMOOTH MUSCLE

Apart from skeletal muscle, you have two other types of muscle in your body, cardiac muscle and smooth muscle.

Cardiac muscle is found only in the heart and is described later in the book. Smooth muscle is found in the walls of hollow parts of the body such as the stomach, intestines, blood vessels and the bladder.

Smooth muscle fibres (cells) are arranged in layers in the walls of these hollow organs. Normally there are two or more layers. The fibres in each layer run in different directions so that they have opposite effects when they contract.

Smooth muscle is also called involuntary muscle. The reason for this is that you cannot consciously decide to make it contract. Instead, it is under the control of a part of the nervous system called the autonomic nervous system. This system automatically controls a whole range of body functions without you being aware of them. These include pushing food along the digestive system after you have eaten, and squeezing urine out of the bladder when you go to the bathroom.

Unlike skeletal muscle, smooth muscle contracts slowly and rhythmically, and does not tire easily.

Bladder wall
The urinary bladder is one of the body's many hollow organs. Its function is to store urine. When it is full, smooth muscles in the bladder wall contract to squeeze urine out of the body.

Smooth muscles in the bladder wall
The bladder wall contains three layers of smooth muscle cells or fibres. The fibres in these layers (left) run in different directions. Each smooth muscle fibre (above) is much shorter than skeletal muscle fibres and lacks their stripes – hence the name 'smooth'.

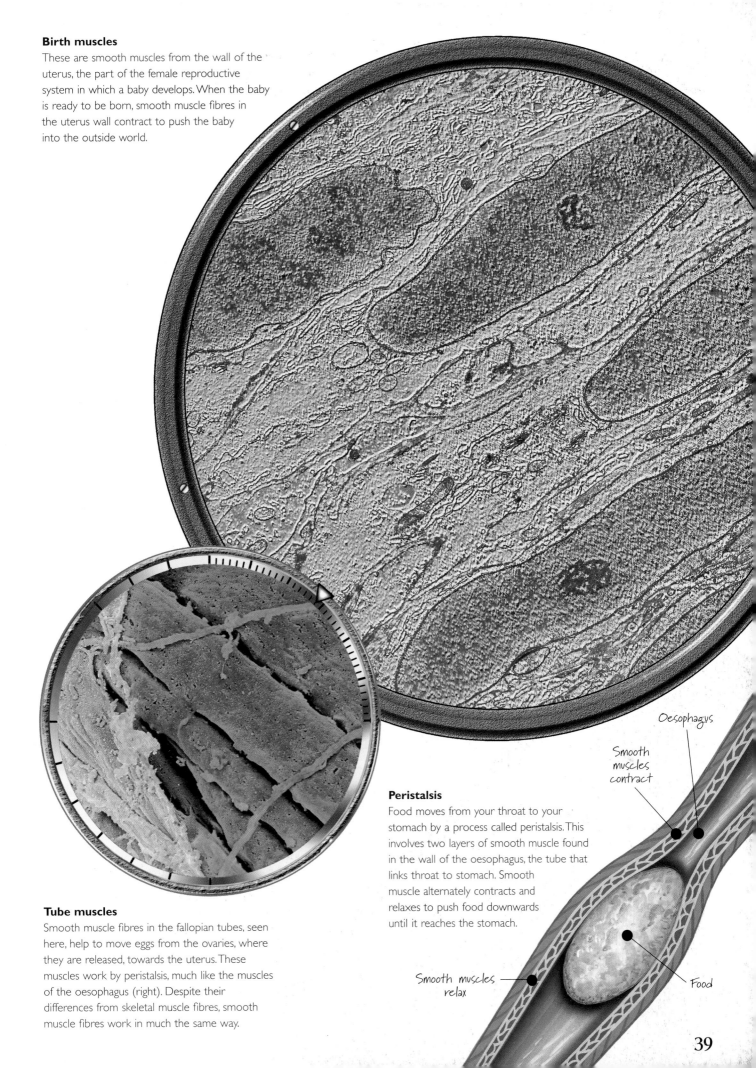

Birth muscles

These are smooth muscles from the wall of the uterus, the part of the female reproductive system in which a baby develops. When the baby is ready to be born, smooth muscle fibres in the uterus wall contract to push the baby into the outside world.

Tube muscles

Smooth muscle fibres in the fallopian tubes, seen here, help to move eggs from the ovaries, where they are released, towards the uterus. These muscles work by peristalsis, much like the muscles of the oesophagus (right). Despite their differences from skeletal muscle fibres, smooth muscle fibres work in much the same way.

Peristalsis

Food moves from your throat to your stomach by a process called peristalsis. This involves two layers of smooth muscle found in the wall of the oesophagus, the tube that links throat to stomach. Smooth muscle alternately contracts and relaxes to push food downwards until it reaches the stomach.

Oesophagus

Smooth muscles contract

Smooth muscles relax

Food

39

CARDIAC MUSCLE

Your heart beats non-stop about 100,000 times each day without tiring. It can do this because it is made of a special type of muscle, called cardiac muscle, that is found only in the heart.

Cardiac muscle fibres (cells) contract automatically to squeeze the walls of the heart inwards, an action that pumps blood around the body. The rate at which they contract is set by part of the heart called the pacemaker. This sends out electrical signals that pass from one muscle cell to another and cause them to contract at the same time.

Nerves supplying the heart do not make it contract: they serve to speed up or slow down the heart according to the body's requirements. When you exercise, the heart beats faster than normal to get more oxygen and food to your skeletal muscles. The nerves supplying the heart are part of the autonomic nervous system, which automatically regulates internal actions without us having to think about it.

Cardiac muscle fibres
Cardiac muscle cells are striped, like skeletal muscle cells, and they have a similar internal arrangement of myofibrils and filaments. Unlike skeletal muscle, cardiac muscle fibres have branches.

Heart strings
The heart strings are tendon-like cords found in the heart. At one end they are attached to the wall of the heart. At the other end they are linked to the valves that ensure blood flows in the right direction through the heart. When the heart contracts, the heart strings stop the valves blowing backwards, like an umbrella turned inside out in the wind.

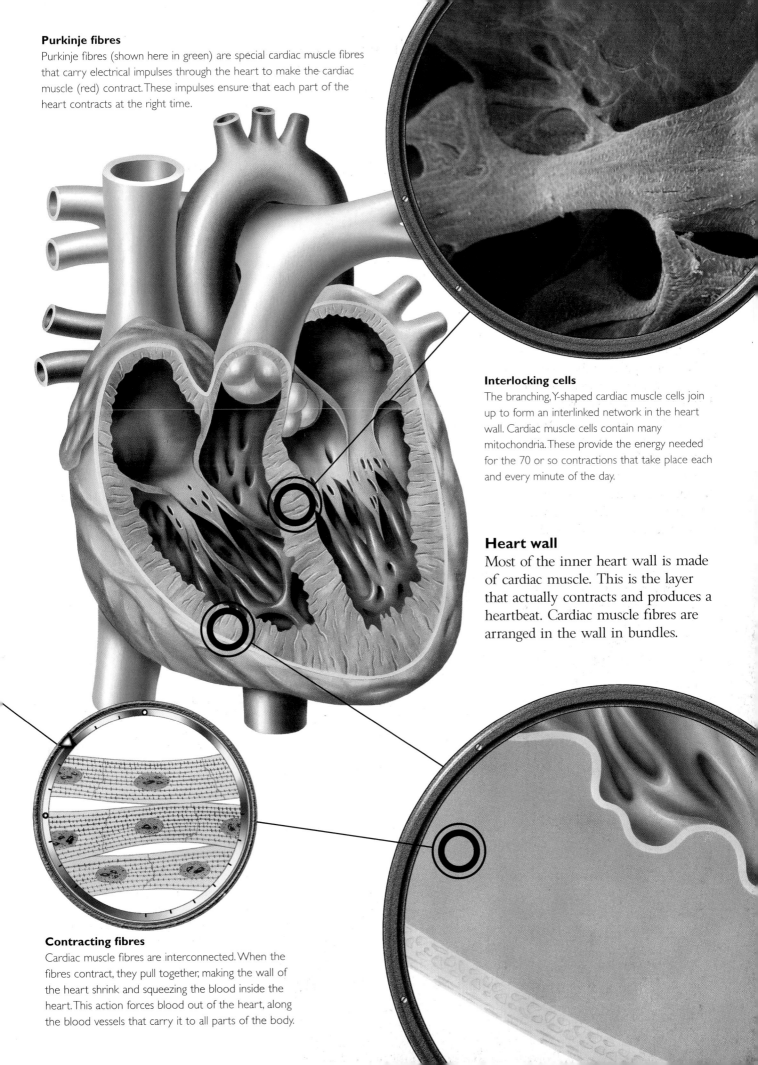

Purkinje fibres

Purkinje fibres (shown here in green) are special cardiac muscle fibres that carry electrical impulses through the heart to make the cardiac muscle (red) contract. These impulses ensure that each part of the heart contracts at the right time.

Interlocking cells

The branching, Y-shaped cardiac muscle cells join up to form an interlinked network in the heart wall. Cardiac muscle cells contain many mitochondria. These provide the energy needed for the 70 or so contractions that take place each and every minute of the day.

Heart wall

Most of the inner heart wall is made of cardiac muscle. This is the layer that actually contracts and produces a heartbeat. Cardiac muscle fibres are arranged in the wall in bundles.

Contracting fibres

Cardiac muscle fibres are interconnected. When the fibres contract, they pull together, making the wall of the heart shrink and squeezing the blood inside the heart. This action forces blood out of the heart, along the blood vessels that carry it to all parts of the body.

MUSCLE DISORDERS

Skeletal muscles and tendons can develop injuries and disorders like other parts of the body, and stop working properly.

Many muscle and tendon injuries are caused by overuse. Others may happen if a person exercises strenuously. In both cases, muscle and tendon injuries should be treated with rest. The risk of experiencing injury during strenuous exercise can be reduced by warming up before exercise. This involves spending a few minutes practising a gentler form of the exercise to be performed, or jogging for a few minutes.

The benefit of warming up is that it increases blood flow to body muscles and makes them warmer. In this state they are ready for action and are less likely to be strained or torn when strenuous exercise begins. Strains and tears are injuries that will heal in time. But there are some diseases of the muscles, such as the inherited disease muscular dystrophy, that cannot be treated.

Tennis elbow

Tennis elbow can be caused by playing tennis or by other activities that use the arm, such as painting or gardening. The tendon that links forearm muscles to the elbow becomes tender and sore because it is overused. Resting the arm can help get rid of tennis elbow.

Repetitive strain injury

This is an injury caused by overuse of one part of the body. It can happen to people who work on assembly lines or who spend many hours typing. As the typist's fingers move endlessly over the keyboard, nerves and muscles in the hand and forearm become sore and make further work painful.

Torn muscle

Sudden movement when playing a sport like soccer can actually tear muscle fibres inside the muscle. This can cause pain, bleeding and soreness. The muscle must be rested so that it can mend itself and make a full recovery.

Torn Achilles tendon

The Achilles tendon links the calf muscles, which bend the foot downwards, to the heel. The Achilles tendon may snap, perhaps when a sprinter (right) sets off from blocks at high speed, or when a squash player turns suddenly. A torn Achilles tendon can be repaired by surgery in which the torn ends are stitched together.

MUSCLE CARE

By looking after their muscles, people can avoid aches, pains, and injuries now and when they get older. Regular exercise and a good diet helps to keep the muscles in good condition and ensures that they are less likely to be injured.

Knowing the correct way to lift heavy objects helps to avoid the back injuries that so often happen when lifting. For people who use computers, or who sit at a desk for long periods, it is important that their desk and chair are both at the correct height, and that their computer screen and keyboard are placed in the right position to avoid straining the body unnecessarily. If minor muscle or tendon injuries occur, there are simple self-help methods that can be used to reduce the pain and to speed up the healing process.

Sitting correctly

Sitting incorrectly at an office desk can cause all sorts of muscular problems and pain. A person who, like this woman, is working on a word processor at a desk, should arrange her work area to minimize back and other injuries.

The chair should be at the correct height and of the right design so that the back is supported properly while keeping the body upright, and the feet are kept flat on the ground. The arms should be parallel to the ground and just resting on the keyboard. The computer screen should be in front of the user so that she does not have to look up or down when working.

Lifting correctly

Lifting heavy objects incorrectly is a common cause of muscle injury. All too often, a person will bend over an object and try to lift it with their legs kept straight. This puts unbearable pressure on the back and can cause strain and tears of the back muscles and tendons.

When lifting a heavy object, you should bend your knees before holding it. Then, keeping your back straight, push upwards with your legs and straighten them in order to lift the object. Make your legs do the work to avoid straining your back.

Rest

If you have a muscle or tendon injury, the best immediate treatment you can give it is the 'RICE' procedure. It is called RICE because you have to Rest the injured part, put Ice on the injury, apply gentle pressure to Compress the injury, then raise or Elevate the injured part.

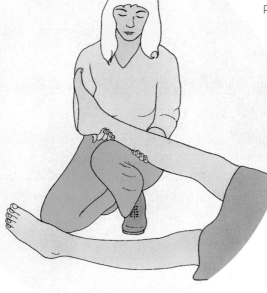

Ice

Just after an injury has occurred, using an ice pack or a cloth soaked in cold water can help reduce the swelling. After an injury, the affected part gets hot as it becomes more sore and tender. Applying something cool – and this could be a pack of frozen food from the freezer wrapped in a cloth – reduces both the temperature and the soreness.

Compression

If the site of the muscle injury is carefully and gently compressed, this can help. It can be done by putting a thick layer of plastic foam or cotton wool around the injury, then tying it – not too tightly – using a bandage. Compression supports the injured part and helps reduce the swelling.

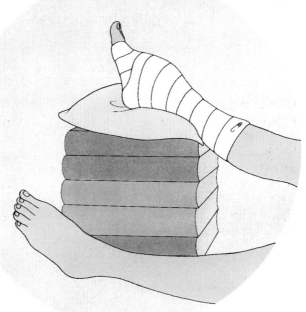

Elevation

Elevation, or raising the injured part on a cushion or other suitable object, helps to reduce the risk of bruising. Bruising is caused by bleeding under the skin. Elevation reduces the blood flow to the injury, and cuts down the amount of bleeding that can occur. So, to treat a muscle or tendon injury, remember RICE.

GLOSSARY

ABDUCTION
Movement that pulls a part of the body away from the body, such as pulling the arm out to the side.

ACHILLES TENDON
The body's strongest tendon, the Achilles tendon links the calf muscles to the heel.

ACTIN
Thin filaments found inside myofibrils. Actin and myosin – the other type of filaments – slide over each other to make the myofibril contract.

ADDUCTION
Movement that pulls a part of the body towards the body, such as pulling the arm inwards towards the body.

ATP
High energy substance that stores energy released from glucose in the mitochondria until it is needed for muscle contraction.

CARDIAC MUSCLE
Type of muscle found only in the heart. It produces the heart beat. Cardiac muscle contracts of its own accord without tiring.

COLLAGEN
Tough but slightly elastic fibres that are found in bundles inside tendons.

DEEP MUSCLE
Skeletal muscles that are located further away from the body surface, below the layer of superficial muscles.

DEPRESSION
Movement that pulls a part of the body downwards, such as lowering the jaw.

ELEVATION
Movement that lifts a part of the body upwards, such as raising the lower jaw.

EXTENSION
Movement that increases the angle of a joint so that bones either side of it move further apart. An example is straightening the arm.

FASCICLE
Bundle of muscle fibres held together by a sheath. A skeletal muscle is made up of many fascicles.

FILAMENT
Tiny threads found inside a myofibril. There are two types of filament – actin and myosin – that slide over each other to make the myofibril contract.

FLEXION
Movement that reduces the angle of a joint so that the bones either side of it move closer together. An example is bending the arm.

INSERTION
The place where the tendon of a muscle is attached to a bone that moves. The opposite of origin.

JOINT
The place where two or more bones meet. Most joints are freely movable.

MITOCHONDRION
Mitochondria are tiny structures found inside muscle and all other body cells. Energy is released from glucose inside the mitochondrion and turned into ATP, a form of energy that can be used by the cell.

MUSCLE
A body tissue made up of muscle fibres that are capable of contraction to produce movement of part of the body.

MUSCLE FIBRE
Name given to the elongated cells found in muscle that are each capable of contracting or getting shorter.

MYOFIBRIL
Microscopic threads found running inside a muscle fibre. Myofibrils contain filaments that cause muscle contraction.

MYOSIN
Thick filaments found inside myofibrils. Myosin and actin – the other type of filaments – slide over each other to make the myofibril contract.

NERVE
A bundle of neurons that carries nerve messages to and from the brain and spinal cord. Nerves reach all parts of the body.

NEUROMUSCULAR JUNCTION
The place where neurons meet muscle fibres. There is a small gap between the neuron and muscle fibre.

NEURON
Long thread-like nerve cells that carry nerve messages – called impulses – to and from the brain and spinal cord. Many messages from the brain are carried to muscles instructing them to contract.

ORIGIN
Where the tendon of a muscle is attached to a bone that does not move. The opposite of insertion.

ROTATION
Movement that turns one bone around or on another, such as turning the head from side to side.

SKELETAL MUSCLE
Muscles that pull on the bones of the skeleton in order to move the body and maintain its posture. Skeletal muscles are under the conscious control of the brain.

SMOOTH MUSCLE
Muscle found in layers in the walls of hollow organs such as the bladder. Smooth muscle contracts without us thinking about it.

SUPERFICIAL MUSCLE
Skeletal muscles that are located near the body's surface, above the layer of deep muscles.

TENDON
A tough cord made up of collagen fibres that connects a muscle to a bone.

THERMOGRAM
A 'heat picture' that shows how hot different parts of the body are, and which parts of the body are releasing more heat than others.

INDEX

Acknowledgements

The publishers wish to thank the following
for supplying photographs:
Michael Abbey/Science Photo Library (SPL)
8-9 (B), 16 (TR), 21 (TR); Biology Media/SPL
6 (CL); Biophoto Associates/SPL back cover
(BL), 9 (CL), 11 (BL); Prof. S Cinti/CNRI/SPL
39 (TR); CNRI/SPL 3 (CR), 6 (TL), 15 (CR);
Gene Cox/SPL 12 (CR, BL); Don Fawcett/SPL
6 (B); Adam Hart-Davis/SPL 19 (L, BR);
Manfred Kage/SPL 18 (TL), 38 (BL), 40 (CR);
Astrid and Hanns-Frieder Michler/SPL 12
(CL); Miles Kelly Archives 4 (TR), 32 (C, BL),
33 (C), 36 (BL, TR, BR), 37 (T, B), 42 (C), 43
(T, B); Prof. P M Motta/Dept of Anatomy/
University 'La Sapienza', Rome/SPL 7, 10 (BL);
Profs P M Motta and E Vizza/SPL 39 (BL);
Philippe Plailly/Eurelios/SPL 13 (TL); Philippe
Plailly/SPL 13 (TL), 40 (BL); D Phillips/SPL 41
(TR); Quest/SPL front cover (CL), 23 (B); J C
Revy/SPL 11 (TL); Rex Features 8 (BL); SPL
front cover (CL, CR), 4 (C), 16 (BL); Secchi,
Lecaque, Roussel, UCLAF–CNRI/SPL 21 (CL);
Pat Spillane 15 (B), 20 (CL, model Wesley
Stevenson), 21 (B, model Wesley Stevenson),
24 (L, model Victoria Beacock), 25 (BL, model
Shoji Tanaka; R, model Wesley Stevenson), 26
(CL, model Wesley Stevenson), 27 (L, model
Wesley Stevenson), 28-9 (model Africa
Green), 30 (BL), 33 (R, model Puspita
Mckenzie), 34 (B, model Puspita Mckenzie; R,
model Wesley Stevenson), 42 (B); The Stock
Market 31 (TL, C).